To Every Truth Its Season

5/14/02

To
Bob –
with great admiration

Hope you do not find
this too presumptuous

Sam

To Every Truth
Its Season

Poems

Sam Seifter

*Illustrations by
Jonathan M. Abrams*

MMII • FITHIAN PRESS, SANTA BARBARA

Published by Fithian Press
A division of Daniel and Daniel, Publishers, Inc.
Post Office Box 1525
Santa Barbara, CA 93102
www.danielpublishing.com

LIBRARY OF CONGRESS CATALOGING–IN–PUBLICATION DATA
Seifter, Sam, (date)
  To every truth its season : poems / by Sam Seifter.
      p. cm.
    ISBN 1-56474-392-6 (pbk. : alk. paper)
    I. Title.
    PS3619.E42 T6 2002
    811'.54—dc21
                                    2001005489

With love and gratitude,

to Eleanor,

my wife of almost sixty years

CONTENTS

Preface / 9

A Principal Uncertainty / 13

The Garden of Our Years / 16

Code Written in a Country Crickyard / 18

Contemplating My Novel / 20

Standing before Hiroshima, 1967 / 22

Cambodia—1969 and After / 26

The Children of Ma'alot / 28

The Austro-Italians, Helly and Ilse,
    in Their Citroën, Take Us For a Ride
        Around Lake Como—Easter, 1973 / 30

Letter to A. on Her Leaving / 35

Arieh Berger / 37

To Nina / 38

Dicentra Bleeding and Hard-pressed / 39

The Pink—Dianthus—The Carnation / 40

Verbena and Salvia / 43

The Word Is Too Much with Us? / 44

Mammalia in Line / 46

Aces High / 47

The Hubble Bubble / 48

Music of the Spheres / 49

Haiku—Evolution / 50

At Jamaica / 51

Summary Delivered at the End of a Course in
    Pathology and Aging / 52

Petrarch Speaks from His Home in Arqua / 54

Wonder in the Spring / 55

Winnegans Fake / 58

Some Brief Notes on "Winnegans Fake" / 62

PREFACE

These selected poems were written occasionally over a period of about forty years. The occasions were visits to places of historical interest, tributes to special persons in my life, and exhibits of pressed flowers prepared by me and Shizuko Takahashi.

The poem "Code Written in a Country Crickyard" is a presumptuous resetting of Gray's "Elegy Written in a Country Churchyard." A *churchyard* can be transformed to a *kirkyard*, which in turn incorporates the spirit of Francis Crick of the historic Watson–Crick structure for DNA.

"The Children of Ma'alot" was written in May 1974, shortly after the unconscionable massacre of schoolchildren of Ma'alot and Safaad in Israel.

The poem about Arieh Berger was written in memory of a great Israeli scientist and humanist. He worked at the Weizmann Institute and died in 1972.

Nina, for whom the poem "To Nina" was written, was a wonderfully insightful and gracious woman of the pioneering generation in Israel. Nina saw poems I had written about others and asked playfully why I did not write a poem for her. So I did. In this poem the Shlomo, of course, is the Solomon of the Song of Songs.

"Aces High" refers to World War I German and American aviators who downed the most of enemy planes. Those were Manfred von Richthofen (1892–1918) and Edward V. Rickenbacker (1890–1973). Their lives were examples of the futility and waste of that war. Although the two airmen were not related, their names become intertwined in this poem.

"Music of the Spheres" remembers two composers, both of whom were also professional organists devoted to the heavens. Herschel became a great astronomer, and Holst had astrological interests. Sir William Herschel (1738–1822) chronicled the skies with a telescope that he had built; in 1781 he discovered the planet Uranus (which he thought at first to be a comet). Gustav Holst (1874–1934) did not discover any planets; instead he wrote music presuming to describe the known ones.

At Easter in 1973, my wife, our friend Betty Rubin and I explored northern Italy. We drove through the Euganean Hills from Padua to Arqua, where Petrarch had lived after returning from France. The poem about Petrarch represents some of my thoughts at Arqua.

Helly and Ilse, about whom the poem "The Austro-Italians" was written, had come to Italy in the 1930s and thereafter lived in Como. Their father had been a well-known Viennese designer–architect; and Helly and Ilse had grown up knowing many of the prominent artistic persons of pre-World War II Austria.

I want to express gratitude to my daughter Madeleine Abrams, her husband, David, my son, Julian, and to my grandchildren, Andrew, Charles, and Rebecca, all of whom appear in these poems in many hidden ways. I owe special thanks to my daughter-in-law, Betsy Seifter, not only for fugitive appearances, but also for overt and important textual suggestions.

Finally, I want to acknowledge my grandson, Jonathan M. Abrams, who illustrated these poems. He worked patiently and with great insight while I hovered over his shoulders. We got to know one another at a new level.

SAM SEIFTER, 2001

To Every Truth Its Season

A PRINCIPAL UNCERTAINTY

One fine day,
in the late defining years of my life,
I allowed my mind
the irresponsible pleasure
of unabridged playfulness,
and leafed through my dictionary
in unaccounted search
for funny-looking words:
words, which when met head-on,
free of guardian qualifiers,
seem quaint and even hilarious.
Towards the end of my quest,
having reached the nether region of words,
I found
yes.

I have not
consulted my psyche sufficiently
to know the funny that is yes,
but I know the finality
that it holds.
Three laughing letters:
first, an hermaphroditic vowel,
then a most certain vowel,
that knows its self,
and finally, a sibilant consonant
that could go on hissing forever,
as though it had begun in Eden
and is working its way through eternity.

This accordion word,
so compressed and enfolded,
holds the affirmation of all the truths
that have arrived, and those that are yet to come.
It is the principal certainty of all we are
and will ever be,
and the verdict that speaks the truth.
It is anagrammatic
in every Odyssey,
and in Ulysses himself,
and is even misanagrammed in Joyce.
Shouted in one sharp Archimedean cry,
or whispered in a Galileian sotto voce,
it can also be a prolonged exhalation
of some exploding truth;
or alternatively
it can sound like Nora–Molly Bloom's
permissing breathless yess,
so full of promise.

In my dictionary,
yes,
so vast in consequence,
needs only four lines
for definition and usage; while
a,
so indefinite an article,
and the first word in my catalog of words,
needs more than half a column.

So there, I thought,
so ends my search for funny words,
ending with the bang of certainty.

And then my eyes
(also brimming with a yes)
advanced three words
in the alphabetic march from
yes.

And there was
yet,
a transformation not to be devoutly wished;
a mutation, a shift in the generic code,
from s to t
(as in the word shift itself).

Gone was the funny,
gone was the certainty;
enter the serious,
enter uncertainty.

And then I knew:
to every truth its season,
to every yes its yet.

𝔗𝔥𝔢 𝔑𝔢𝔴 𝔜𝔬𝔯𝔨 𝔗𝔦𝔪𝔢𝔰

NEW YORK, FRIDAY, FEBRUARY 9, 2001

TINIEST OF PARTICLES POKES
BIG HOLE IN PHYSICS THEORY

15

THE GARDEN OF OUR YEARS

In the garden of our years
No season goes unflowered,
No earth denies its yield.
In the garden of our years
The soil is self-renewing,
Never begs for nurture,
And holds its demiurge.

In the garden of our years
The original zinnias soon went to seed
But new varieties were easy bought.
And the morning glory is still there
Although we pretend it must be weeded
While secretly sabotaging our own
Annual efforts to root it out.

Begonias are bye-gone,
As they should let be.
But the phlox remains
On both our houses
In the garden of our years.

Here the rose has never lost its prim,
Nor its comely blush.
Nor has the cosmos lost its captive charm
To draw the bumbling bee.

In this garden of our years
Dahlia lances always are in flower;
And each year their tuberescent roots
Increase our store of next year's pleasure.

Geraniums are always relevant
In the garden of our years:
With multifloral carpels
Each tipped by glabrous awn.

The yucca soars its stalk
As though Goethe's Weib draws it ewig up.
No flower dares to droop its head
In the garden of our years.

The balsam of Gilead
Soothes our passage through
The crowded blossomed garden path
Down which we kindly lead.

The poison ivy knows with whom it deals
And exercises trifoliate self-restraint
As it stops short beyond
The garden of our years.

The shapes are multi-formal
And the colors make their quantum leaps.
But every play of shape and hue
Has stemmed from two
In the garden of our years.

CODE WRITTEN IN A COUNTRY CRICKYARD

The curly tails are those of parting DNA,
    The double strand unwinding into complements;
Thus the species upward plod their endless way,
    And live their lives which are a base existence.

Beneath these rugate walls, the membrane's shade,
    Within the nuclear chromosomal heap,
Each in a narrow cell forever laid,
    The purine forebears of the helix sleep.

Let not cynicism mock man's useful toil,
    His homely joys, for everything is planned:
So when the doublet shuffles off this mortal coil,
    The code remains within the single strand.

The boast of heraldry, the pomp of pow'r,
    And all that beauty, all that wealth commands,
Arise alike in that stripping hour:
    The paths of glory lead but from the strands.

Perhaps in this cistronic spot, in sweet repose,
    A gene is pregnant with celestial fire:
Phosphor, bases and sugar of ribose,
    Hold everything to which we can aspire.

Thus information lies within the ample chain,
    Rich with coils which time does e'er unroll
(Relieving then the full genetic strain),
    Ensures the genial current of the soul.

Though full many a chain may bear the purest gene,
    In dark unconscious turns of helix hid,
Should many a flower be born to blush unseen,
    Don't lay this failure to the twisted Id.

Far from the madding crowd's ignoble strife,
  The sober bases never learned to stray;
Along the cool annealing vale of life
  They kept the matching tenor of their way.

On some fond code the parting chain relies,
  Some pious bonds the leaving strand requires;
E'en from each base the best of nature's ties,
  Hydrogen atoms send out connecting wires.

THE EPITAPH

Here lies the code within the DNA.
  The nucleotidal affairs of man return,
Each time transcribed in message RNA:
  In this our nature's copy is eterne.

NOTE: Thanks to Thomas Gray and William Shakespeare for use of their lines.

CONTEMPLATING MY NOVEL

Books stand on my shelves,
some erect, some awry,
like tombstones tooled for eternity,
but weathered even in these few years.

My library is a cluttered cemetery
where coffins cradle brittle words
left by spirits long since fled;
where Geist is really ghost.

Each leaflet box
is so many reverential years
of someone's reaching to be remembered.

Then should I work to stack a book
in this gravesend?
to be forgotten alphabetically
or by some arrogant filing code
that presumes to know
what occupied my mind?

To tell the truth,
I feel like Mozart in his thirty-sixth year
without ever having had his thirty-fifth
or thirty-fourth or any other count-down year.
I am Mozart without having been he:
which is to say,
I have revealed nothing
nor have I been an instrument of revelation.

I think my library
shall be safe from me.

STANDING BEFORE HIROSHIMA, 1967

Here in this city
of seven ashen rivers
and seven river beds of silted hidden crimes,
here in this city
new-grown with people
like a forest razed and sown again,
where I look at faces
but fear to read the recessed minds
lest falsely I credit them with outcroppings
of shadow guilts and remembrances
of my own remorse:

Here in this city
glorious overhead with sunlit sky
yet always underneath a stalked and tethered cloud,
here in this city
whose agony made the world forever an ephemeron
(until its time should be no more forever)
and changed the mythic revelation of Armageddon;
here I feel the caterpillar creep of anguish.

But here in this city, especially,
I know that absolution is cheaply bought
by quickly changing gasps of disbelief
into accents in a rush of verse.

Here of all places
why make a poem?
Why write immortal words?
To move a world
to whom Hiroshima may be a Sunday rotograph
like templed tombs of ancient pharaohs?
Is Hiroshima a monument or mausoleum
for airborne pilgrims to stand beside
and win release with sanctifying guilt?
Here, why carve a testament?

Here I know what happened
after millennia of coded faiths, injunctive tablets,
impassioned psalms and fraternal pledges.
Here it came to pass,
and the host, whose shadow fell and killed,
held itself the most edified and codified
and compassionate.

Life is great with grand deceits;
so it is written in the fabric
there must be poems to the last searing breath,
alleging faith while knowing how it ends.

(Yet nature is more wonderful than life;
it gave life to life and wove
its own instructive ironies into the tissue.
So it is that the eye informs the brain
which then compels the eye to weep at what it sees:
but what it sees the brain has already willed.)

Anyway, you must have faith!
Yet all the faith is there,
drawn in line and written in word,
couched in phrase and spoken in praise,
sung in hymns and oozed in silence:
it is all there
flung across the centuries
with conceit that it is greater,
less vulnerable than humankind itself:
and even more immortal.

If only you should take the time
to tune the ducts
and codify the shame,
then you too shall be poet and priest
in the lineal descent to Hiroshima.

Because it is not that life divides
so there are those who do the deeds
and others to repent.
Not that simple,
nor so simple that in each there is
this perfect symmetry in space
and this equanimity of parts in time.

Standing small and desolate before Hiroshima,
before the large and most perplexing works of man,
a lonely Blake-like figure before the universal night,
a repenter taking renouncing vows
and wanting desperately
in the way of poets and priests
to think for all that,
for all the words and tears and faith,
the world's transformed.

LEST WE FORGET • NANKING, 1937

HIROSHIMA, 1945 • LEST WE FORGET

CAMBODIA—1969 AND AFTER

In the land of the Khmers
in the land of the lakes
we came that December
before our troops in the Spring
started the end of it all.
Now who knows in Kampuchea
to cry, Oh Weeping Judaea!
or to tremble with hope?

In the land of the lakes
in the villages near Siem Reap
the beautiful Khmer people
lived in stilted huts
above the wet rouge earth
in strange symbiosis
with the silent dead past
of their ancestral Angkor Wat.

In the land of the waters
the sacred Bo Tree fig
that gave birth to the Buddha
sent out long limbs,
spread its cheese-like bark,
and patiently over the centuries
strangled the Hindu statuary,
the temples and the palaces,
with intruding strong roots.

Now in the land of Khmer Rouge
how quick is the noose
that ties off the past?
how slow the new death,
how quick the new birth?
how painful the death
how painless the birth?
and mostly, shall children
ever know to smile again?

THE CHILDREN OF MA'ALOT

Children of Ma'alot,
battered children of our hope,
your ordeal is over
and in the hill beds of Safaad
you rest in gentler cover
than any we could give in life.

Children of Ma'a lot,
guide us clearly,
for our grief is too confused;
and there is peril
that our only legacy to you
could be the vengeance we will do.

Children of Ma'alot,
you are also the children of Theresienstadt,
of Maidanek-Lublin, Mi Lai, Belfast,
Mozambique, and a crowded geography
of death in dust-dry villages,
quick-dug ditches, huddled schoolhouses,
gas and napalm chambers,
rifled huts and cobbled streets;
and, lest we forget,
soul-consuming refuge camps.

Children of Ma'alot,
and all the others,
there was no escape in your time,
although for each many thousand years
of generations of children
had grown and multiplied
to bring you to this point and then to death.

Each child returned
to the stones of Safaad
or the sands of the Sahara
or the smog over the Ganges
is the cruel cut-off
of so many centuries of hope.

And now begins again
the endless wait
for the generation
that can kill the hate.

THE AUSTRO-ITALIANS, HELLY AND ILSE, IN THEIR CITROËN, TAKE US FOR A RIDE AROUND LAKE COMO— EASTER, 1973
(a letter of thanks)

Kennst du das Land
where the white Citroën booms
and curves along right and left shores of Como?
And
Connais tu le pays
where the orange blossoms bloom—
but white like orange blossoms should?
And
Knowest thou the fair land
where, on one Palm-less Sunday,
and whatever is the Monday that follows,
Helly and Ilse sprang from our unconscious
(for they must always have been with us)
to lead us on like two urging angels
in the upper frieze of a long-ago painting,
to view Paradise?
And then to lead us sadly away,
although there were yet,
as in Walther's song,
Helly, like Eva, im Paradies,
and Ilse too.

"Comum meae deliciae."
PLINY, Ep.I.3.

What associations were loosed
as conversation leaped with every turn in the road
and cove of the lake!
And later we exchanged stories
as we drank tea from their Bobba's Meissen,
and talked with poorly joined connections
of Hans Sachs (remember his house?),
and of Beckmesser who almost stole the Meistersinger Prize.
And then we Weilled away the time
as we talked of Kurt.
(Wo weilest du?)
You were Dukas's Sorcerer's Apprentices
(but we drank politely from the Guilded teacups,
not from the sorcers or saucers,
as might have Alice's Mad Hatter).

And, then, in the Plinys' Como place,
there was a plinitude of good things,
Younger and Older, including a platitude
of traditional Easter Columba
(a dove sculptured in coffee cake,
which, when we dissected away her spread of wings,
was poor Columbina).

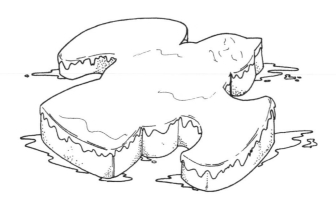

And we felt like William Tell
as we rowed in mixed metaphor across Lake Como
(really drawn by ferry swans);
but this time, instead of chasing us,
the Austrians were safely in our boat.

And then more conversation.
Take Pittsburgh's William Steinberg, for instance,
or turn the Stein over and
take Leonard Bernstein, for instance,
whose name is preserved Forever in Amber.
Yes, take Leonard, who conducted Bellini,
because Bellini had conducted himself so poorly!
Casta Diva! and Pasta, too!
(Remember that Pasta was Bellini's starchy prima diva?)
And in our talk, as we ran over the centuries,
we did not forget Alma Mahler,
and Jackie O.,
and poor Maria, Dame of the Callas!

PASTA DIVA

And, so, when the lilacs
next threaten to bloom in the doorway,
we shall return to Como
like the ever-returning Spring;
and there shall be sweet roses and wine,
and Helly and Ilse,
waiting on the shore,
waving our return,
as last we saw them waving farewell.
Good women drawing us ewig on,
so that we can end this letter
of grateful thanks,
as we began, with Goethe,
a Fausto evento.

LETTER TO A. ON HER LEAVING

You are worth a poem,
or many poems,
with all the modulations that words can brush,
without burden of weight of touch,
on matters of joy and sorrow.
In a moment of headiness
one might say that you are worth a poem
by a celebrating Lope or Heine or Garcia
in another time when writers were allowed to deal,
whether with lightness or brooding,
with things that are called the spirit.

We don't speak of competence
(for which no poems should be written).
We don't speak of saintliness
(for which poems are redundant).
We speak of all those other things
for which poems always have been written,
but made so singular in you.

We talk of your serenity
(not without self-doubts
and cascades of inner turmoil),
affecting all those who stand still to witness.
Your calmness is almost that of the convent
but drawn by a different path,
and having no residue of the conventional.

We think warmly that
you have not set yourself apart.
You agonize with suffering,
and become enraged by injustice.
And yet, it is the agony of the agonized,
and the frustration of the enraged,
that change is not easy made.
No criticism, then, that you
have made a contract of personal goodliness.
A certain sadness of our life is
that the wrenching of the heart
and the sorrow of the mind
have often made us philosophers and saints
where wise people and heroes are needed.

There is no leaving without regret.
Things unsaid, forms observed, time ignored
as though there would be no day of parting.
In the scale of things reparations are hardly possible,
Rarely made, and probably unimportant.
But yet regrets are poignant,
and for this we have said enough.

ARIEH BERGER

In our time
we knew a man who walked gently among us,
who shook the upper slackness of our minds
but calmed the ground beneath our uncertain steps.

We knew a man
whom we were proud to love with unconscious ease—
because, without performing,
and just by being,
he was the inner person we yearn to be,
naked of the tangled shroud
that complicates us to the world.

He had to be our teacher;
and his lesson was that going the path of truth
is the greatest truth that we shall know
in our relay passage through the long generations.
In this way
there can be no conceit
nor arrogant self-deception.
Nor in him were there these things.

In our time
we knew this man,
and took comfort
that tranquil people can yet be born;
and that when giants walk
the earth need not tremble.

TO NINA

This morning as I plowed the deep
Of unadorned and silent sleep,
I was wakened by a temple bell,
The glorious voice of Philomel.

Ah, Philomel, a maid of Athens,
Whom now we know as Philomena;
And whose name is love of song,
Nightingale, but really Nina.

All my youth I heard songs of birds
the Spanish swallow, La Golondrina,
The Spanish dove, La Paloma,
And then the Neapolitan Nina.

NIGHTINGALE

Yes, the Neapolitan Nina,
Likened to the turtle dove of Shlomo,
Whose voice in Spring is clearly heard
Throughout the land of Palestina.

Pergolesi glorified his Nina
While others sang of Columbina
(Except for pious Palestrina),
But I will only praise this Nina.

SWALLOW

TURTLE DOVE

DICENTRA BLEEDING AND HARD-PRESSED

In the garden I've set the stage,
a digitalis just left of center
to support a bleeding heart
which with smug textbook wisdom
I keep far removed
from the hemorrhagic sweet clover.

The arc-swung central branch
is strung with candy hearts
in diminuendo,
each fibrillating in the breeze
with a belly full of closet wind
like a true-blue ventricle.

Foxgloves and Dutchman's breeches!
an unlikely pair of any wear,
fit only to distress a tailor
unless, like here, he puts them to the press.

Such botanic cleverness
and therapeutic wit,
but really nothing more nor less
than an offbeat fit.

BLEEDING HEART

FOXGLOVE

39

THE PINK—DIANTHUS—THE CARNATION

Praise be the pungent pink!
Dianthus, the flower divine;
Incarnation of the gods.
(O, Celeste Aida: forma divina, mistico serto di luce e fior…)

It has a saw-toothed crown,
So like a lion's mane;
Indentured petals,
Yet has no toothache pain.

Its secret remedy is home-grown,
And flows through floral veins;
No mere lymph-borne curative metals
Anticipate its pains.

CARNATION

So praise to its oil of clove!
Essence, the fragrance divine:
That is the ichorous liquor
(O, ma Carmen: gardait toujours sa douce odeur...)

No licorice, this oil of clove,
But ether of the gods;
An esthetic anesthetic
To soothe the jaw of Jove.

So, praise be the pungent pink,
Especially its unguent clove!
No cloven ungulate, the devil incarnate,
But rather the carnation of Love!

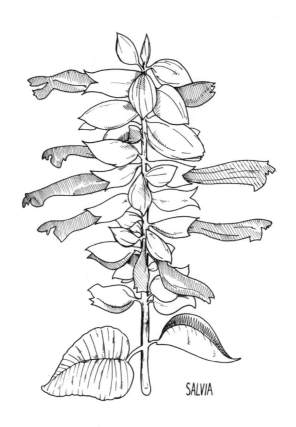

SALVIA

CARDINAL FLOWER

VERBENA AND SALVIA

Let us celebrate a Novena
for the nine fast colors of verbena:
scarlet, rose, salmon, magenta,
indigo, lavender, purple, lemon and white.
The list is long and quite verbose,
the punctuation really commatose,
and the language, if not the leaves, so tomentose.

So hail, verbena!
Your flowered crown forms a halo,
and you border on the saintly,
because in the garden you are shelved just below
(infra red) St. John's Fire, the salvia, our salvation,
and the scepter of your coronation.

So hail, salvia!
The scarlet sage!
Newly minted wisdom borne on aeromatic spires,
way beyond the aspirations of any cathedral.
You are no mere dogma like the cardinal flower,
no germanic question like the rock-breaking saxifrage,
and no impertinence like the inconstant sassafras.
And so we ask:

Who is Salvia? What is she?
That all our saints command her?

SASSAFRAS

43

THE WORD IS TOO MUCH WITH US?

Without W.S. Gilbert,
Sir Arthur Seymour Sullivan,
weary and ill-at-ease,
was seated one day at the organ,
and struck and lost a chord
with the sound of a great Amen:
then he wrote The Lost Chord.

Without Sherlock Holmes,
Sir Arthur Conan Doyle,
weary and in need of a change,
was seated one day at his sleuthing desk,
and found a world
long-lost in the great Amazon:
then he wrote The Lost World.

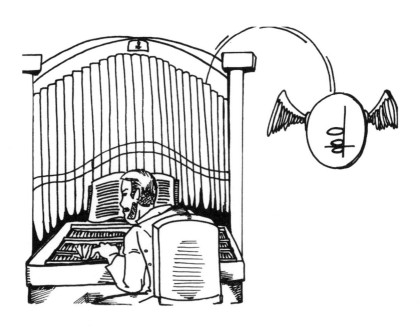

From that we learn
that there are chords within chords,
words within words,
and worlds within worlds.

But beyond all those withins,
within the word world
is the word word,
which, when removed,
leaves a lonely l;
and that is what a world without words would be—
an aspirated hell.

MAMMALIA IN LINE

(as it was in the early 1800s)

The English and the French,
Divided by a trench,
Have (in common!) some royal things,
Especially how they grow their kings.
Both have laws of primogenitalia,
Telling how to relegate their regalia.
So, from cetacean provinces,
They choose their royal princes:
Indeed they honor Wales and Dauphine
When they crown the next of kin.
So, in England, succession goes to the Prince of Whales;
And, in France, it is Le Dolphin who prevails.

Ye gods, and bigger fishes!

ACES HIGH

A poem for World War I—German-American Relations

Manfred v. Richthofen   Edward V. Rickenbacker

Richtenofen   Richtenbacker

Richtofenbacker   Richtenbachtofen

Rückenbaker

Rückenofen   Rickenofen

Richthofen   Rickenbacker

(May both Resound in the Heavens with Beethoven;
May both rest in the Underworld with Offenbach.)

THE HUBBLE BUBBLE

Sonnet about eternity written on a challenge by Madeleine
(at Carl's and Myrna's apartment, 1962)

The universe expands, the stars grow red,
So like a rose with petals reaching out,
Whose puckered lips are the celestial spout,
Whose heart is white, to whose rim the fire has fled.
Oh mighty Newton in your earthly bed,
Oh matchless Einstein who struck the first great doubt,
Your phosphorescent spirits now fly without.
You were the start and end: white heart, rim red.

deSitter sat in Amsterdam and thought;
And while he dreamed he chewed Bazooka gum.
And, lo, a bubble blew! He watched it growing,
His mouth, his nose, in gummy substance caught.
And from this vision he plucked a choicest plum:
The universe is a bubble that God is blowing.

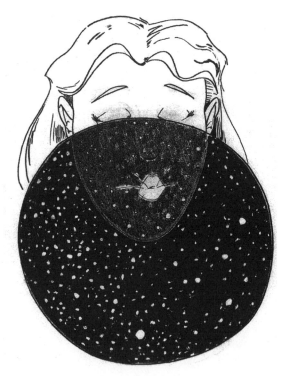

MUSIC OF THE SPHERES

On once more looking into Keats's
"On First Looking into Chapman's Homer"
(written in four-sevenths of a sonnet)

In England, about a century apart,
In Keats' apt phrase, two watchers of the skies,
Both organists but yet, to no surprise,
Were also writers in the tonal art.
Watching a new planet swim into his ken,
Herschel found *Uranus* in its own ellipse.
Holst, then, hoping to escape eclipse,
Wrote *The Planets*—like Cortez misplaced in Darien.

HAIKU—EVOLUTION

Written in Dr. Noda's Tokyo house, dining room overlooking
a garden full of shrubs, flowers and toads

Inside the warm house
we talk of evolution.
Outside, toads evolve.

AT JAMAICA

At Jamaica a redoutable tout
Ran horses that suffered with gout.
Because of their tophi
They never won trophi:
Their gout was atrophic no doubt.

SUMMARY DELIVERED AT THE END OF A
COURSE IN PATHOLOGY AND AGING
Sponsored by the National Institute on Aging,
Cornell University, 1972

According to our teachers' scheme,
Things are seldom what they seem;
Lobules are hepatic fiction,
Kidneys have immune addiction.

Lupus erythematosus
Is simply DNA nephrosis.
(So, if you suffer immune adherence,
Better watch your renal clearance.)

Basement membranes always thicken,
In man and ape but not the chicken.
Older brains have tangled lesions,
Especially those from Melanesians.

Kuhn the Third then gave the schema
That older lungs have emphysema.
And yet, as though in proud defiance,
The older lungs have great compliance.

Now juxtameddling with Kashgarian,
Farber showed Promethean carrion:
Implying then that most pathology
Can be found in Bullfinch's Mythology.

Then Van Lancker patched things up
With a wad of enzyme glup.
And proved to us with wondrous ease
That repair can cure, and cause, disease.

And Russfield, with the charm of Carol Channing,
Cheered us with her careful scanning,
Ending with an adeno-hypothesis (à priori),
Which is better than adeno-hypophysis (à posteriori).

Jones, springing from a primate base,
Showed us mice of every race:
Yellow, black, and tutti frutti
Age as well as plain agouti.

Then with marvelous expression,
Sokoloff spoke of aged genuflection:
How potted joints lose dynamic—
It all appeared psychoceramic.

Stehbens jeered at cholesterol,
Passed it off as fol-de-rol.
Terry ditto lipofuscin;
And ceroid wasn't worth discussin'.

And in a week we've reached senility,
Lost some neurons and virility.
And Coleman, with the greatest 'scope,
Convinced us that there is no hope.

And if you think that things relax,
Now come Pitot, Leader, Flax;
Not to mention Dante (Virgil) Scarpelli,
Who sounds like he will fill our belli.

PETRARCH SPEAKS FROM
HIS HOME IN ARQUA

These hills, these rocks, these stones, this sand, this dust,
These walls, this court, this arch, these stairs, this bay:
On these, these rocks, I built my words to stay
When vectored time should lose its forward thrust.
An arc of stone, a covenant of trust,
I saved for you the songs that lit my day,
That you should know our work, our love, our play,
In this golden age stained through with rust.

But don't believe that everything endures,
Outwitting death with sweet and comely cures.
Unless a rooted change transforms relations,
Your poems will start with mortal intimations:
These mounds, these ruins, this fragile earthen crust,
This grass, these weeds, these petals in the dust.

PETRARCA
(1304-74)

WONDER IN THE SPRING

Every Spring
I count the last year's dead and lost,
dream-fixed
at the irretrievable silent film
that spills unsprocketed
on the sometimes lazy always crazy
curves of uncontaining time,
like moëbius strips in crazy daisy chains,
or unhemmed amoeban pseudopods
into unresisting space,
leaving tangled movie strips
hung in sky
at once as great and small
as the selenic silence that fills an atomsphere:
a sky of so few highs and lows
that the reeling river spills not flows.

For the Autumn self
who lives to count the past year's claim
there is the sad memory of someone
having been and gone,
as though there really had been no act of leaving,
but some other inexplicably left behind
by a God whose mystery is that he moves
with no potential drop;
or who does not move at all.
(There is no way to tell
because God's God
has put him in an almost windless sky.)

Yet every year is heavy
as I count my loss.
And in the Spring, when I move fingers
tenderly on the abacus of my mind,
with the wonder that once again
my universe has turned,
and the ground is turning,
and I wonder that I am here
to make the vernal count;
and wonder to whom will pass the call
another Spring.
And would it matter except
that it is all a thing
for wonderment?

And yet
I do not mean to play the meaningless game
of find the meaning;
and willingly concede the bigger cosmic play.
And I'm passive in any hare and tortoise race,
so paradoxical in the real world:
the invented paradox
that one half-truth and yet another
sum to greater than nothing-but-the-truth.

So I leave the bigger things to God
and self-anointed emissaries
whose accounting properly begins
with all the Januaries.
Instead in Spring
I start again the shorter human course,
the unmeasured race,
the active pace,
of Pacem in Terris.
(I find my reading of the Latin imperative
more moving than any Hellenistic halving
that forever baits the goal.)

So why should I care,
in the Spring,
that stars also die and become nebulous?
My loss was cut so deep
there should be no counter-cure
in diverting wonder that a phoenician Crab
was born a thousand years ago
as witnessed in a Chinese ledger
and mirrored in telescopic sweeps at Palomar.
No doubt this should heal and comfort:
to know in deed if not in spirit,
how great is God the maker,
God the shaker,
and taker of everything small and large;
the changer of living to dead
and back again—if you believe.

Our God which is unleaven
is our God the prestidigitator
(save his Sistine finger),
the quick-change artist,
jealous of his performance,
creator of his audience,
so that they shall always wonder
in wondrous wonderment.

I wonder.

WINNEGANS FAKE

Isolde Meets Her Fate

To the Kernwall coast from Airinlandt,
along the Kurvenwall,
Wagnerian histail bindem,
full of brangewine,
came Richard the Lyonasse,
Reichheart of the royal mange.
The kinks were full of murkiness,
and all was Marked with
intesterniecine wharfare
among the piers where plowedman
and plied and played the pompiss.
Helaine, helass! the lily,
made the astalot,
lancedalot, dancedalot,
duncedalot, duncedascot,
and no wallfleur.
When Twistran lapsed in the doorway,
when Assault assended with steep ascent,
there wereno kinks,
there werenoblasse
and all obleeged
in those Sterne oldendays
of Obadais
on Tristan Shandys shores.

Shesolt herseul herseulf
to no Boyweulf but to Mefisteulf,
but thatwas innuther tail
innuther taime, before the Fleud
had flowed innuther taime
innutherdate.
(Sorry! We have mixen the fat with the lean,
the bedder with the Margarine,
the crown with the jewel,
the crone at Cronewall
with the Fusty legendermain. Sorry!)

When Murlin walked around the walls
and Teichos stalked around the walls,
and Canis caulked,
who then would catterwaul
and cawl and crawl
and haul and hawl and howl
in the middennoon and aftherloon?
The mid of Astalot?
the lid of Astamot?
Did they givealot for the Dam
or gievadam for the Lot?
Sartainly not!
Were theynot a saddned tristed lot?
an ellova lot?
eggs ovathedam?
Camalot! O Tryste!
O Morte! O Vissi! O dArthe!

The errow has fleuwn
and hit its Mark;
treushot the beult,
threugh to the tarkget.
When Jock Robin last
to the Markget a grail of warter,
a Pursiful o brownale,
a bucketful o wry,
the shirereeve of Puttinham
wellcomelied
the hooden bow of Robincock.
Many shafts were held within his Quiniver, ivermore.
The sherf was sharf in Nothinghim;
and neeragain on cornterrain
did robinrain—
but did tristanreign?

Now tween Errinland and Angletear
there sweeps a sea with boom and brush.
O contradicture!
that the Angles have no kinks nomore;
in murrie Inkland there are no manarchs,
no rouleurs, just sofruns.

The inks are rawyell blue
from crowngall made
from nutgall shade.
The kappas fled the cappéd Kinks
and left behind the royal Inks.

So weeps the sea, a wee,
the angry irish sea,
for the unmarked queen.
So quiver the quells and quiet nomore,
and Paristellsus the sea issalt.
The murmids weep
but not for her the Fleur
but for their finnie seulfs—
which half no release?
For them
what matter no kinks no crowns
whenno rings to brink the annonue?
No Scylla no sully no CribIdis.
No division in Gallus.
No gully in gally, no allée.
No Gutmunde getrude to Telletrude.
Only a muricle could save amoracle.
Let Isolt the squirmaid amorsononcle
in Venis
in the circle of Sans Mark Place,
but alas,
demyrrhmaid cant!
She can churn the oras

and scale a scylli barkerole
as she skims the dogesplice,
but no forrard wall no backarole
assin Issole.
O beautiful face without a foss:
fossaken middenhead with maidenhid.

And wails the sea against the wall
for Daedend quail,
the queen, the tristed self,
the Oyrisch Kindt, the Wehward,
the Cornish sylph.
Insted,
Melot should quaff the Dram on Attic shores.
Raze the Ruf and rail the Heavns,
but nomoreletsbe melotramatic.

Blast ard the Rich;
dead art the wickt.
Those who enter the Liszts
have no Cosa complain.
Said von Bulof, no Boyweulf he,
frischwehtderwind,
and Hinterreise with Sickfreed.

SOME BRIEF NOTES ON "WINNEGANS FAKE"

"Winnegans Fake" is not meant to be a parody of the work by James Joyce, but rather a bow to certain aspects of Joycean writing. Also, these notes are a broad guide to the poem and not a detailed key to its many allusions and nuances.

Tristan, in the Wagnerian version, brings Isolde to Cornwall from Ireland to marry his uncle, King Mark. Tristan is accompanied by his faithful attendant, Kurvenal. Isolde is looked after by Brangaena, who is transformed here to Branntwein (Brandy), the provider of the fateful love potion.

All becomes murky with uncle–nephew–aunt–niece internecine struggles. The face of Helen from Ellas appears, and her name is fused with Tennyson's Elaine, the Lily Maid of Astolat. Helen, like Isolde, had been carried off. Even Duns (dunce) Scotus works his way in as one who might bring reality to the individual characters of this story.

Now we jump to Laurence Sterne's *Tristram Shandy,* who coincidentally had an uncle, but this one named Toby. Obadiah, a mysterious character who weaves in and out of that novel, is called on to mark time. Then, because the stream of consciousness is so well developed in Sterne, we let it get carried away on Joyce's wings of aria; and so we mix it up with *Faust* and the *Jewel Song.*

The environment is magical with Merlin. The castle walls and ramparts are brought in as the Latin *mur* and the Greek *teichos.* Dogs howl at the moon and bark at the sun, and there is Astarte and betrayal. That brings us to the betrayal of Tristan by his fellow knight Melot. We then lead into the story of another betrayal with Floria Tosca singing her aria, "Vissi d'arte," in the presence of the tormenting Baron Scarpia. One has to remember that the opera *Tosca* ends with the heroine flinging herself over the ramparts of the Castel Sant' Angelo. This is truly the *Morte d'Arte.*

More interplay then follows concerning the Arthurian Percival and the Wagnerian Parsifal and the Holy Grail. Robin Hood and the Sheriff of Nottingham appear with all kinds of sexual and anal-intestinal developments in dark recesses. All is made blue and black with different kinds of inks made from crown gall, including royal blue.

The Isolde-Mark relationship was probably inconsummate, and represents a source of frustration expressed in the great ventral–dorsal anomaly of the mermaid. This leads to the frustration of Elsa and Lohengrin, the Knight of the Holy Grail. They must lose all their future happiness because Lohengrin is bound to tell-the-truth when questioned by Elsa (which he should not have been). References are then made to the evil Telramund and his wife Ortrud in the same legend. Ortrud becomes merged with Gertrude of *Hamlet*. Thus Ortrud is complicit in the transformation of Elsa's brother to a swan, and Gertrude is implicit in the transformation of her first husband to a ghost.

Then we go to Venice where the second act of *Tristan und Isolde* was completed by Wagner in 1858. We observe relevant events from the Doge's Palace, and we hear the Barcarolle from Offenbach's *Tales of Hoffmann*.

Lastly, we come to commentaries about Wagner himself. First, there is the concern that he may have been a son, born out of wedlock, of a Jewish actor. Then there is his involvement with Cosima Liszt as he won her from the seemingly compliant conductor, Hans von Bülow, who had conducted the first performance of *Tristan und Isolde*. Finally, there is reference to the winter musical celebration of the birth of Wagner's son with Cosima. Thus we have *The Siegfried Idylls*, with memories of Siegfried's *Rhine Journey*. As the story ends, we hear the recurrent song of the seaman sung at the beginning of *Tristan und Isolde*, and quoted early in *The Wasteland* of T.S. Eliot:

Frisch weht der Wind
der Heimat zu:—
mein Irisch Kind,
wo weilest du?